THE STORY OF SPACE

SPACE PIONEERS

Steve Parker

A+

Smart Apple Media

Published by Smart Apple Media, an imprint of Black Rabbit Books
P.O. Box 3263, Mankato, Minnesota 56002
www.blackrabbitbooks.com

Produced by David West ☂ Children's Books
6 Princeton Court, 55 Felsham Road, London SW15 1AZ

Designed by Gary Jeffrey

Cataloging-in-Publication Data is available from the Library of Congress.
ISBN 978-1-62588-080-2

CSPIA compliance information: DWCB14FCP
011014

9 8 7 6 5 4 3 2 1

All images courtesy of NASA except: p5tl, Mr.Minoque; p6t, Bundesarchiv, p6m, T5C. LOUIS
WEINTRAUB; p8l, Vokabre Shcherbakov; p15tl, ElChristou; p18tr, Lobanov Andrey; p25br,
NASA/Bill Ingalls; p28 all, Virgin Galactic; p29tl, Space X, p29m, Ken Ulbrich

CONTENTS

US Space Shuttle orbiters played vital roles in building the International Space Station. But the Shuttles, pioneering reusable spaceplane designs, would prove costly in both resources and human lives.

INTRODUCTION

The dream of spaceflight has been with us since the 17th century. Johannes Kepler decoded planetary motion, and Isaac Newton formulated force, motion, and gravity. Another great visionary was Konstantin Tsiolkovsky, an early 20th-century schoolteacher who described practical methods for getting into space.

To achieve those dreams, it took two World Wars, hard-won engineering know-how, and a dangerous rivalry between two great superpowers. And it took guts—the personal courage of pioneer astronauts who rode their towering rockets into the unknown.

US astronaut Alan Shepard takes a bow on the deck of rescue ship USS Lake Champlain, *May 5, 1961. The first American, and second person, into space, he should have launched seven months earlier. But his Mercury capsule, in the background, was not ready.*

ROCKETS INTO SPACE

The first space rockets were dreamed up by theoretical visionaries, hobbyists, and the designers of weapons of war.

ROCKETEERS

Late-19th-century writers Jules Verne and H. G. Wells were the first to popularize the idea of spaceflight. Their works inspired many, including Konstantin Tsiolkovsky, a Russian schoolteacher with an unquenchable thirst for knowledge. In 1903 Tsiolkovsky formulated how a craft might actually leave Earth by attaining escape velocity. He also suggested the fuels to achieve this would be liquid oxygen and liquid hydrogen.

Victorian science fantasy author Jules Verne imagined going to the Moon in a capsule fired from a giant gun.

Tsiolkovsky worked out that a rocket would need to accelerate in stages to escape Earth's gravity.

Tsiolkovsky was a theorist. It was American physicist Robert Goddard who made the first liquid-fueled rocket. Goddard's *Nell*, launched in 1926, reached an altitude of just 41 feet (13 m), but it proved the concept. Goddard devoted all his free time to building bigger and better rockets, but he could not get funding from the US government.

Rather than in the US, Goddard's work was noticed more in Germany, which in the 1920s was gripped by a rocket craze. The leading pioneer was Herman Oberth (center) who published the best-selling book Ways to Spaceflight *in 1929. Oberth helped found rocket "societies" where physicists and engineers created more powerful rockets. One of Oberth's leading lights was young aristocrat Wernher von Braun (second from right).*

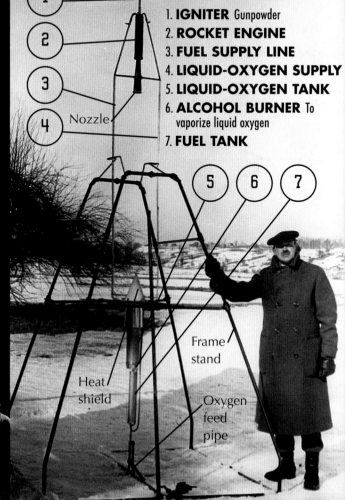

GODDARD'S NELL

1. **IGNITER** Gunpowder
2. **ROCKET ENGINE**
3. **FUEL SUPPLY LINE**
4. **LIQUID-OXYGEN SUPPLY**
5. **LIQUID-OXYGEN TANK**
6. **ALCOHOL BURNER** To vaporize liquid oxygen
7. **FUEL TANK**

Nozzle

Frame stand

Heat shield

Oxygen feed pipe

Germany's A4 rocket—the world's first spacefaring ballistic missile—was successfully test-launched in late 1942. The A4 featured innovative chemical-fueled turbo pumps and gyroscopic guidance systems. It was the culmination of nine years of research and development.

Up to **3,225 V-2 ROCKETS** were **launched** in **COMBAT**, **most** aimed at **MAJOR CITIES**.

SUPERSONIC VENGEANCE

In 1933 the Nazis rose to power in Germany and outlawed civilian rocket societies. Rocket scientist Wernher von Braun decided to work for the military rather than give up research.

In World War II, missiles did not become important until 1942. By then Germany's plan to take Europe was failing. Von Braun's A-4 missile was readied for mass production and renamed V-2 (*Vergeltungswaffe* or "Retaliation Weapon"), but did not become useable for another two years. As Germany retreated in 1944, V-2s were unleashed against England. But it was too little, too late.

In 1945, Germany was invaded from east and west. Both Americans and Russians were keen to get their hands on V-2 technology. Von Braun (seen here in a cast) and his team deliberately surrendered to the US Army, which also captured their materials.

Postwar, German scientists were offered work designing missiles for the US. As they tested captured V-2s, they began to probe the edge of space. A V-2-derived two-stage rocket called Bumper reached 244 miles (393 km).

The US and Soviet Union first competed in a race to design missiles for nuclear weapons. The space race did not start until the surprise launch of Soviet satellite Sputnik 1 (left) in 1957.

ANIMALS IN SPACE

The world's first sub-orbital astronauts were two Russian dogs, Dezik and Tsygan, launched in 1951. In the early space race, animals were used to gauge space's hostility to life.

INSIDE SPUTNIK 2

1. **NOSE CONE** To be jettisoned
2. **SCIENTIFIC INSTRUMENTS** For investigating short-wave radiation
3. **SPUTNIK RADIO TRANSMITTER** Aerials bent to make a framework
4. **LAIKA'S CABIN** Complete with porthole

Soviet space dogs were fitted with pressure suits. The effects of microgravity (weightlessness) on living tissues were unknown.

SPACE HOUNDS

Soviet Premier Nikita Khrushchev was keen to follow up *Sputnik 1* with another "spectacular." Sergei Korolev, the genius behind Sputnik's R-7 launch rocket, sketched a plan to use a backup rocket to send the first living organism into orbit.

Dogs had long been part of Soviet testing, being calmer than monkeys. A small mutt named Laika ("Barker") was chosen. Within a month the capsule, *Sputnik 2*, was ready. On November 3, 1957, Laika blasted into orbit. But a rocket malfunction caused overheating. Laika managed just six orbits before she perished.

Laika's cabin had oxygen, water, and food. But with no time to design an escape system, it was destined to be a one-way trip.

10 P.
РОССИЯ
RUSSIA-2010

50 ЛЕТ
КОСМИЧЕСКОМУ ПОЛЁТУ БЕЛКИ И СТРЕЛКИ

In 1960 Belka and Strelka became the first earthlings to return safely from orbit. They traveled for a day in Korabl-Sputnik 2 ("Ship-Satellite 2"). It was a test flight of the Vostok series of craft that would take the first human into space eight months later.

Life support

"We did not learn enough from the mission to justify the death of the dog."
Oleg Gazenko, biomedical specialist and Laika's trainer

The US's most important animal astronaut was Ham, a chimpanzee. He rode in a Mercury capsule atop a Redstone rocket on a sub-orbital proving flight on January 31, 1961.

Ham

Flight couch

When a helicopter arrived to recover Ham's capsule, it was capsized and sinking. However, when winched onto the deck of USS Donner, Ham emerged happy and unscathed.

WHERE MONKEYS BOLDLY GO...

In the US press, Laika was ridiculed as a "Muttnik." But American scientists had launched mice and monkeys into space since 1949. NASA favored monkeys because of their physical similarity to humans. The first to survive spaceflight were two monkeys, Miss Able and Miss Baker, on May 28, 1959.

NASA needed to know if an astronaut could operate controls under the severe g (gravity) forces of lift-off and in the microgravity of space. Chimpanzee Ham was selected for Mercury-Redstone 2—a fully equipped tryout for the human-rated Mercury capsule. Malfunctions plagued the flight, the rocket accelerated too fast, and cabin pressure dropped. Ham's ride showed Mercury was not ready.

> **Recent ANIMALS** launched into **SPACE** were **MICE**, **GECKOS**, and **GERBILS**, on Russia's *Bion-M1* capsule in **2013**.

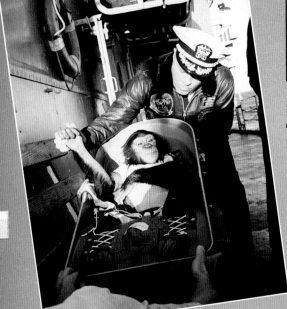

Miss Baker, one of the US's earliest space pioneers, held a model of her Jupiter AM-18 launch vehicle. Miss Baker died at age 27 in 1984, having become the oldest known squirrel monkey.

HUMAN SPACEFLIGHT

The Soviet Union dominated the early space race with their powerful R-7 rocket. By 1961 they were ready to launch a human into orbit.

Vostok spacecraft

3rd stage

Core-stage rocket

1st stage main rocket

1st stage boosters (4)

An innovative design, the Soviet R-7 had a main engine surrounded by a cluster of four boosters. This allowed it to lift far heavier payloads than the US could manage.

A NEW TYPE OF CRAFT

OKB-1, the Soviet space agency, began designing and constructing space capsules. Yuri Gagarin, age 27, was selected for flight from a group of six jet fighter pilots rigorously tested at astronaut training camp. Gagarin's craft was a pressure sphere mated to an instrument module, powered into orbit by a three-stage rocket. The entire sphere was coated with protective material that would burn away on reentry. On April 12, 1961, *Vostok 1* soared upward—and to a place in history.

Architect of the Soviet space effort was Sergei Korolev. Originally an aircraft designer of humble origins, he spent six years in prison under Stalin's repression before working on ballistic missiles.

INSIDE VOSTOK 1

1. **MAIN (DESCENT) CAPSULE**
2. **ASTRONAUT** Lies prone, fastened into ejector seat
3. **INSTRUMENT MODULE** Ringed by nitrogen and oxygen gas bottles for life-support, retro engine (hidden) at rear
4. **THIRD STAGE ROCKET** Boosts *Vostok* into orbit before falling away

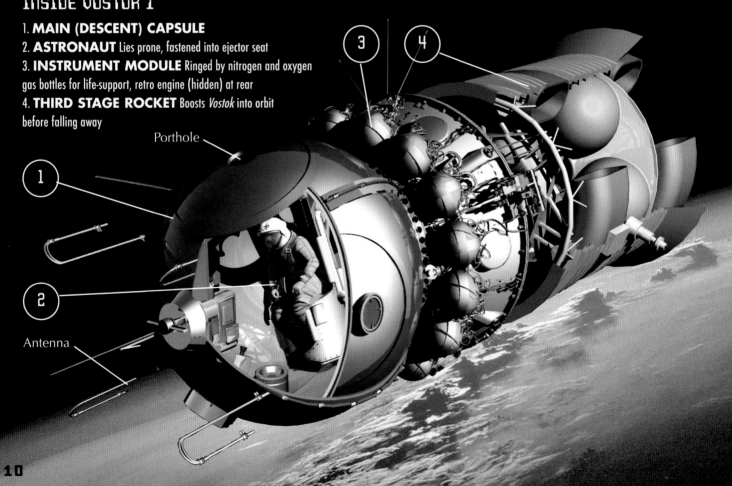

Porthole

1

2

Antenna

Gagarin, the "little eagle" (shown preflight), was the perfect height to fit inside the rounded capsule.

INTO THE BEYOND

After 11 minutes *Vostok 1* exhausted all its stages, which fell away. The shroud had gone too and, peering out of a porthole, Gagarin radioed: "I can see the Earth... everything is good!" Wasting no time, the Soviets announced the first man in space to the world's press. As Gagarin came round again, it was time for reentry.

Gagarin's **SPACEFLIGHT lasted 108 MINUTES**, enough **time** to make **ONE complete ORBIT** of **EARTH**.

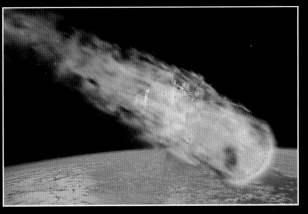

Gagarin's reentry was anything but smooth. A cable tethered to his instrument module remained in place, causing the whole burning spacecraft to yo-yo uncontrollably. At last the cable burned through, ensuring triumph rather than tragedy.

ANXIOUS SECONDS

The craft spun around, fired retrorockets to brake and drop out of orbit, and detached its instrument module. Agonizing minutes ticked by at Baikonur Cosmodrome in the Kazakhstan desert. At 4.5 miles (7 km) high, the escape hatch blew off the falling capsule. Gagarin's ejector seat rocketed him clear and automatically deployed his parachute.

The Soviets believed in equality of the sexes. On the sixth Vostok mission, June 16, 1963, Valentina Tereshkova became the first woman in space.

The Huntsville Times

Man Enters Space

'So Close, Yet So Far,' Sighs Cape

Soviet Officer Orbits Globe In 5-Ton Ship

Maximum Height Reached Reported As 188 Miles

THE MERCURY SEVEN

Begun in 1959, the US's Mercury space program was a characteristically American endeavor—intrepid, thorough, and executed on an industrial scale.

ASTRO PILOTS

Seven manned Mercury flights were planned. They began with ballistic (straight up and down) missions on existing Redstone and Jupiter rockets. More than 500 test pilot candidates were whittled down to a pool of 11 who had the "right stuff." From these, seven were chosen.

The seven chosen Mercury astronauts were all ex-test pilots: three from the US Air Force, three from the Army, and one from the Marines.

The Mercury spacecraft was one-third smaller than Vostok, its instruments integrated inside a cramped capsule. Like Vostok, it was intended to be fully automatic. But manual controls were added when astronauts objected to being merely helpless "passengers" in flight, especially if an emergency occurred.

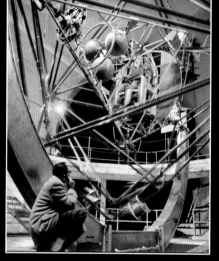

Mercury astronauts' training began on a "multiple-axis space test inertia facility," or gimbal rig. It simulated the expected maneuvers of spaceflight.

The first ever launch of a (unmanned) Mercury-Redstone malfunctioned. The escape rockets fired, leaving the capsule stuck atop the fully fueled rocket—which luckily did not explode.

Escape rockets

MERCURY CAPSULE
1. **ANTENNA HOUSING** Includes drogue parachute
2. **PARACHUTE HOUSING** Main and reserve chutes
3. **ASTRONAUT COUCH**
4. **HEAT SHIELD AND RETRO ROCKET PACK (HIDDEN)** Heat shield designed to boil away, removing heat on reentry

Control panels

The first manned Mercury mission, Mercury-Redstone 3, slowly rose from the launch pad on May 5, 1961—just 23 days after Gagarin's historic flight.

FIRST AMERICAN IN SPACE

Alan Shepard was selected to go first, before John Glenn, Gordon Cooper, Scott Carpenter, Virgil Grissom, Walter Shirra, and Deke Slayton. Delays kept Shepard waiting four hours before his capsule, *Freedom 7,* finally embarked on its short "hop" 116 miles (187 km) up and back.

Weightless for five minutes, Shepard viewed Earth through a periscope and manually maneuvered the capsule around for reentry.

Retrorockets test-fired before the capsule descended in a fireball through the atmosphere. Just 15 minutes long, the entire mission was broadcast live on TV for maximum public impact.

At high altitude, a drogue chute expanded the main parachute for a safe landing in the sea. Shepard and Freedom 7 *were then recovered by Navy helicopters.*

This view of Earth was snapped by remote camera during Freedom 7's sub-orbital flight—which was watched on TV by 45 million Americans.

Shepard, who died in 1989, was a born leader. He had a reputation for being a somewhat temperamental individual.

After **years GROUNDED** with an **EAR disorder, SHEPARD** went on to **command** a **MOON** mission, **APOLLO 14,** in **1971.**

13

ROUND AND ROUND

The Mercury program proceeded with one more sub-orbital flight until the USAF's mighty Atlas rocket was ready to loft a capsule into orbit.

The senior personality and charismatic hero of the Mercury flights was John Glenn.

DOWNS AND UPS

On July 21, 1961, Mercury-Redstone 4 blasted skyward carrying Gus Grissom sub-orbital. The mission went according to plan until splashdown. Explosive bolts triggered too soon, releasing the escape hatch and flooding the capsule. To add to NASA's woes, on August 6, *Vostok 2* astronaut Gherman Titov orbited Earth for a whole day!

Like Redstone before it, Atlas was tested with unmanned and animal-crewed capsules. Astronaut John Glenn followed chimp Enos as the first Mercury human in orbit. Teething troubles with Atlas and the weather delayed the launch until February 20, 1962. Then *Friendship 7* was lifted 165 miles (265 km) high.

Liberty Bell 7, the second manned Mercury capsule, sank soon after splashdown. Its astronaut, Virgil "Gus" Grissom, was lucky to escape drowning.

MERCURY-ATLAS ROCKET

1. **MERCURY CAPSULE**
2. **ATLAS MISSILE BODY**
3. **VERNIER ROCKETS** One each side with moveable nozzles for attitude correction
4. **BOOSTERS** One each side of a central sustainer rocket, designed to fall away

① ② ③ ④

Glenn enters the hatch of Friendship 7. Last-minute problems included the hatch itself, which had a broken securing bolt.

As Glenn soared over the Indian Ocean, he had a breathtaking view of the Sun setting behind Earth.

Retrorocket pack

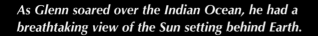

An onboard movie camera recorded Glenn during every moment of his historic flight.

"I SEE FIREFLIES!"

Flying into the rising Sun over the Pacific, Glenn reported seeing mysterious glowing particles swirling outside the capsule window. (These were later discovered to be specks of ice on the craft, warmed and dislodged by the Sun's rays.)

Glenn fired his thrusters to turn the spacecraft. But automatic yaw control (left-right movement) began to malfunction, forcing him to steady the capsule manually into the second orbit. More worryingly, a sensor indicated his heat shield and landing cushion were loose.

Mission control advised Glenn not to jettison his retropack as normal during reentry, and keep the vital heat shield in place. Descending after his third orbit, he was treated to an extra fireworks show as, outside, the retropack burned up.

After Friendship 7 *came* Aurora 7 *and* Sigma 7. *The last Mercury mission was* Faith 7 *with Gordon Cooper. He completed 22 orbits on May 15, 1963.*

Cooper tried out NASA's first attempt at "space food."

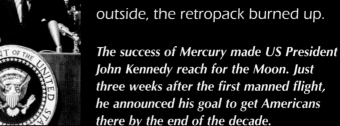

The success of Mercury made US President John Kennedy reach for the Moon. Just three weeks after the first manned flight, he announced his goal to get Americans there by the end of the decade.

The **ATLAS rocket** has **undergone CONTINUAL development** and still **LAUNCHES** spacecraft **today**.

GEMINI

The followup mission to Mercury was designed to hone astronauts' maneuvering skills in orbit using a bigger "twin" spacecraft—Gemini.

Gemini astronauts were seated side by side with doors opening directly to space. Gemini was designed to allow Extra Vehicular Activity (EVA), or spacewalking.

A "FLYABLE" SHIP

Gemini was the first spacecraft able to change its orbital level, or altitude, in flight. It was also the first to accommodate multiple crew.

A modular spacecraft, Gemini comprised a two-crew reentry module (similar to a scaled-up Mercury), a retrograde module, and an equipment module housing life support, fuel, fuel cells, and batteries. The retrograde and equipment modules were fitted with small thrusters for orbital control. Cockpits were laid out like aircraft flight decks, befitting the Gemini astronauts' role as space pilots.

In October, 1964, the Soviet Voskhod 1 (left) took the first multiple crew into space, beating the Americans by five months. When Gemini launched, it was on the advanced Titan missile-based rocket (right).

Gemini capsule

TITAN II

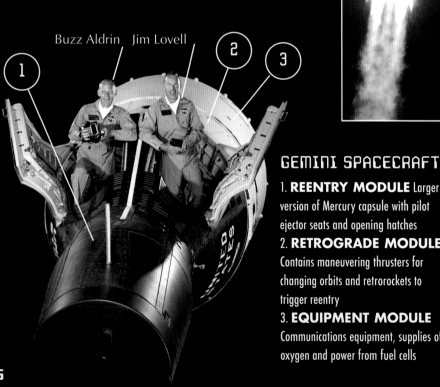

Buzz Aldrin   Jim Lovell

1   2   3

GEMINI SPACECRAFT

1. **REENTRY MODULE** Larger version of Mercury capsule with pilot ejector seats and opening hatches

2. **RETROGRADE MODULE** Contains maneuvering thrusters for changing orbits and retrorockets to trigger reentry

3. **EQUIPMENT MODULE** Communications equipment, supplies of oxygen and power from fuel cells

The tradition of NASA mission patches began with Gemini 5. *The design by Gordon Cooper for his eight-day pioneering mission featured a Conestoga wagon.*

Astronaut Jim Lovell carried his life support pack to the gantry before the launch of Gemini 7.

RENDEZVOUS IN SPACE

The Gemini missions were crewed by a mixture of Mercury veterans and inexperienced astronauts. *Gemini 4* saw the first US spacewalk. But precision orbital maneuvers did not begin properly until *Gemini 5's* marathon eight-day science-based mission.

GEMINI 7

On December 15, 1965, the first rendezvous maneuver of manned spacecraft took place. *Gemini 6A* boosted up to the orbit of *Gemini 7* and drifted to less than 1 foot (30 cm) away. The astronauts exchanged written messages through the windows.

After reentry, Gemini capsules splashed down, like their Mercury predecessors. Gemini 3 *pilot Gus Grissom wanted to name his craft* Titanic. *He was overruled so he named it* Molly Brown *(who survived the* Titanic *tragedy) instead.*

Gemini 6's original mission had been to dock with an unmanned Agena Target Vehicle (ATV). When the ATV exploded on lift-off, Frank Borman and Jim Lovell of Gemini 7 *suggested the Gemini 6 crew rendezvous with their own mission instead. The renamed* Gemini 6A *was crewed by Walter Schirra and Thomas Stafford.*

GEMINI 6A

Docking sight ——

GEMINIs 8 to **12** undertook **increasingly AMBITIOUS** docking **MANEUVERS** to **prepare** for the **Apollo MOON SHOTS.**

SPACEWALKING

The success of Gemini rattled the Soviets. To keep ahead in the space race, they adapted Vostok capsules as Voskhods, for multiple crews—and to send a man out of the craft, to "walk" alone in space.

The Soviets developed an EVA suit by adding an extra layer to their standard flight suit. The Berkut ("Golden Eagle") suit had a life-support pack on the back with 45 minutes' oxygen. Heat, moisture, and waste gas were vented into space by a relief valve.

VOSHHOD 2

1. **ASTRONAUT**
2. **VOLGA AIRLOCK**
3. **SPARE RETROROCKETS**
4. **COMPRESSED AIR BOTTLES**
5. **INSTRUMENT MODULE**

Main retrorockets

A STICKY MOMENT

Voskhod 1 crammed three men into a Vostok sphere. *Voskhod 2* had an inflatable fabric airlock for the EVA (Extra Vehicular Activity) or spacewalk. Pavel Belyayev commanded and Alexey Leonov prepared for EVA. They launched on March 18, 1965. On the second orbit, Leonov pressurized his suit and climbed into the airlock, soon emerging to float on a 16-foot (5-meter) tether.

Leonov soon had difficulties moving. His suit heatèd and ballooned at the joints. Unable to pull himself back in feet-first, he tried head-first but got stuck. In a snap decision he opened his suit's relief valve to deflate—at the risking of boiling his blood. At last he bent his legs inside and sealed the airlock, exhausted but very relieved.

Leonov was celebrated as a superhero in his mother country.

Leonov's intrepid spacewalk lasted 10 minutes and was filmed by a movie camera fixed to the airlock.

"Coming back in was the saddest moment
of my life."
Astronaut Ed White on his spacewalk

NASA devised a pressurized, gas-fed, Hand-Held Maneuvering Unit (HHMU) for its first spacewalkers.

STEPPING OUT

On June 3, three months after Leonov's EVA, NASA astronaut Ed White pulled the latch of his egress hatch in *Gemini 4*. The latch did not budge. Fortunately, his partner James McDivitt knew how to jiggle the faulty spring. The hatch opened wide to space. White raised his oxygen gas "zip gun" and jetted outside, quickly reaching the end of his 15-foot (5-meter) umbilical tether.

Twice more, White jetted between the spacecraft and the tether's end. Easy! He used the HHMU to pitch up and down and yaw left and right. He was having fun. Then the gas ran out. A radio glitch had blacked out Mission Control from Earth until McDivitt reconnected. "*Gemini 4*, get back in!" growled CAPCOM (Capsule Communicator) Gus Grissom.

Ed White's FEAT gained him **PROMOTION** to **APOLLO**. He was **TRAGICALLY KILLED** in the **APOLLO 1 FIRE**.

White used the excuse of taking more pictures to extend his spacewalk. When finished, he had to pull on his tether like a rope to get back in.

SOYUZ

Soyuz was originally designed as a Moon ferry. But as the Soviet Moon effort fell apart, Soyuz became Russia's premier general-purpose spacecraft.

The Soyuz launcher was based on the tried and tested R-7. The core stage housed a more powerful engine to lift the heavier craft.

UNITY

Sergei Korolev conceived Soyuz ("Union") as a pioneering docking spacecraft. But fatality on the *Soyuz 1* test flight (and on US *Apollo 1*) prompted caution. On October 30, 1967, two unmanned Soyuz, *Kosmos 186* and *Kosmos 188*, made the first automated space docking.

The pioneering human mission came on January 16, 1969, when *Soyuz 4* joined with *Soyuz 5* at 136 miles (219 km) up. With no connecting tunnel as yet, the two transferring astronauts of *Soyuz 5* donned spacesuits and floated across. The first ever manned spacecraft docking was completed—nearly two months before the US.

Soyuz spacecraft had no windows for a forward view. They used a periscope viewfinder and radar rangefinding to line up for docking.

Boris Volynov, in Soyuz 5, endured a scary reentry that nearly burned through his escape hatch. Then his capsule failed to fire retrorockets. The hard landing broke his teeth!

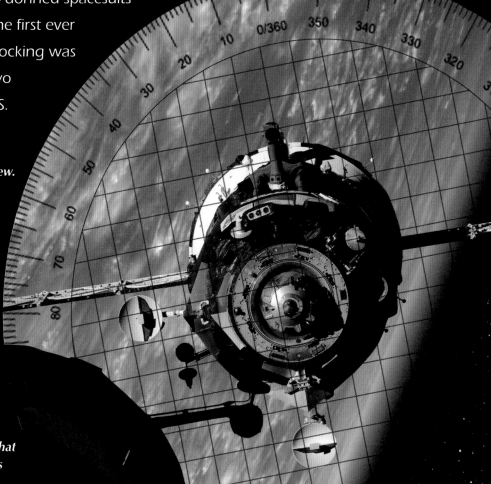

The last ever Apollo journey was during the Apollo-Soyuz Test Mission (ASTP).

HANDSHAKE IN SPACE

By 1972, Cold War tensions between the Soviet Union and the US had eased enough for a first joint space mission. An Apollo spacecraft crewed by Thomas Stafford, Vance Brand, and Deke Slayton would dock with a Soyuz 7K-TM flown by Alexey Leonov and Valery Kubasov.

The political goodwill mission took three years to organize. Critical was a docking module that married the different-sized mechanisms and atmospheres of the spacecraft. The crews also took language lessons and learned each other's technology. On July 17, 1975, east and west successfully came together. They blazed a trail for the multinational space missions of today.

Maneuvering thrusters

1

2

3

APOLLO-SOYUZ

1. **APOLLO SERVICE MODULE**
2. **APOLLO COMMAND MODULE** Also the descent capsule
3. **DOCKING MODULE** With custom-made connecting mechanism
4. **SOYUZ ORBITAL MODULE** Storage and laboratory facilities
5. **SOYUZ DESCENT MODULE**
6. **SOYUZ SERVICE MODULE**

4

Porthole

5

6

Veteran astronaut Alexey Leonov greeted US's Thomas Stafford at the docking module threshold.

Maneuvering thrusters

Solar array

SOYUZ craft still **operate TODAY**. **PROGRESS**, a fully **AUTOMATED** Soyuz spacecraft, **FERRIES supplies** to the **INTERNATIONAL SPACE STATION**.

THE SPACE SHUTTLE

With the Moon race won, NASA returned to its longstanding dream. It planned a fleet of cheap, reusable spaceplanes to carry parts into orbit for a space station.

The final Shuttle plane ended up much bigger than planned, to carry military payloads that helped to offset the cost of the project.

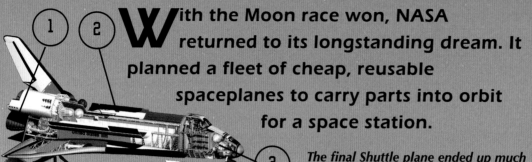

Liquid oxygen Liquid hydrogen

SPACE SHUTTLE

1. **ORBITER MAIN ENGINES**
2. **ORBITER PAYLOAD BAY**
3. **CREW COMPARTMENT**
4. **MAIN FUEL TANK** Liquid oxygen and hydrogen, disposable
5. **BOOSTER ROCKET** Solid fuel, collected and reused

On April 12, 1981—20 years after Gagarin's historic flight—orbiter Columbia lifted off on STS-1 with an empty payload bay and a crew of only two.

SPACE TRANSPORT ONE

The Space Transportation System (STS) featured a Shuttle orbiter riding a huge external fuel tank (ET), with twin detachable-recoverable Solid Rocket Boosters (SRBs) to help lift-off.

At mission's end the orbiter flipped over and fired retroengines before rolling back to re-enter. Special ceramic tiles protected the underside from reentry heat, enabling it to glide in for landing. After reconditioning, it was ready again. The first four orbiters in space were *Columbia, Challenger, Discovery,* and *Atlantis.*

The **INAUGURAL launch** of the **SHUTTLE** was **also** the **FIRST** time **all** of its **SYSTEMS** were **tested TOGETHER**.

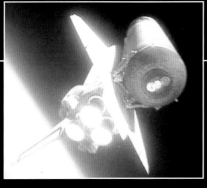

The camera on a falling booster
rocket shows how the orbiter flies
inverted beneath the ET. With the
tank gone, basic orbital flight is
inverted—looking down on Earth.

ORBITER SYSTEMS

1. **MANIPULATOR ARM**
2. **BAY DOOR RADIATORS**
3. **OMS POD** Orbital Maneuvering System
—liquid-fuelled main rocket and Reaction Control
System (RCS) thrusters
4. **RCS NOZZLES**

ORBITER ASCENDANT

STS-1 was the culmination of seven
years' development and testing. Even
now, the Shuttle remains the most
technologically complex machine ever
built. At 28 miles (46 km) up, the spent
SRBs fell away to drift into the sea by
parachute. The orbiter's three powerful R25 engines—the first
and only reusable rocket engines so far—continued to power
the craft to 70 miles (113 km). Here, the empty tank
separated to fall and burn up in Earth's atmosphere.

Veteran astronaut John Young led
STS-1. He had flown Gemini and
been to the Moon.

Now in spacecraft mode, the orbiter opened
its two bay doors with their radiators
that cool the ship. Young and
Crippen spent the next two and a
half days (37 orbits) at 190 miles
(306 km) up, checking all the
systems.

Window onto
payload bay

Main engines

Main maneuvering
rocket

STS-1 arrived home safely at Edwards Air
Force Base, California—the first ever
wheeled spacecraft landing.

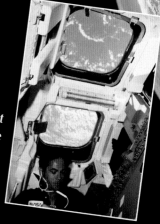

Here STS-1 astronaut
Crippen floats above
Earth, seen through the
cabin roof. The remote
manipulator arm
controls are at his left.

Originally **budgeted** at **$200
MILLION, over** the **SHUTTLE'S
LIFETIME** the **average COST** per
launch was **$1.35 BILLION**.

GREAT SHUTTLE MISSIONS

The Shuttle remained in use for double its intended lifespan. Over 135 missions, it hauled freight and hosted landmark in-orbit construction and repairs.

STS-9 launched Spacelab, a microgravity habitation and experiment pod housed in the orbiter bay. Spacelab was used on 25 missions.

SPACE UTILITY

The Shuttle Remote Manipulator System (SRMS), or Canadarm, was carried on 50 shuttle missions. On April 6, 1984, *Challenger* took off on the first in-orbit repair mission to fix NASA's *SolarMax* satellite, using Canadarm to grapple the satellite. Shuttles also carried into orbit three of NASA's Great Observatories, beginning with the Hubble Space Telescope in 1990. Hubble was serviced by Shuttles five times, getting new cameras, instruments, solar panels, and gyroscopes.

On STS-7 in 1983, Sally Ride became the first American woman into space. Shuttle flights opened up space beyond test pilots to include scientists and engineers.

The **experience** of **SPACELAB** was **INVALUABLE** to the **designers** of the **ISS**.

In 1984 on STS-41B, Bruce McCandless performed the first untethered spacewalk using a gas-propelled backpack.

Canadarm

Payload bay

STS-61, the first Hubble servicing mission, turned into an epic 11-day operation. New instruments were fitted to correct a flaw in the telescope's main mirror. Here Story Musgrave rides Canadarm towards Hubble.

> *"The Space Shuttle marks our entrance into a new era."* US President Ronald Reagan, 1982

On mission STS-71, June 27, 1995, Atlantis *rose toward the Russian space station Mir. It carried a docking pod to attach to Mir's Kristall module. It was NASA's 100th manned space mission.*

Spacelab module

Orbiter Docking System (ODS)

DISCOVERY, the HARDEST WORKING shuttle, accumulated 365 DAYS in SPACE.

STS-88 saw the beginning of the ISS. With US connecting module Unity positioned in the bay, astronauts on endeavor used Canadarm to pull Russian cargo module Zarya slowly towards it.

On STS-128, in 2009, Discovery brought the Multi-Purpose Logistics Module (MPLM) Leonardo to the ISS. It was a large pressurized container for taking materials to and from the station.

On October 29, 1998, for STS-95, 77-year-old John Glenn returned to space after 36 years, as the oldest astronaut in history.

HEAVY LIFTING

Finally, on December 4, 1998, the Shuttle began to fulfill its original purpose of putting together an orbiting space station. The first International Space Station (ISS) mission was flown by *Endeavour*, a new Shuttle built from spare parts to replace the lost *Challenger*. It took 13 years and over 35 more Shuttle visits to finish the ISS. Internationally constructed modules, trusses, and solar arrays were hauled up 229 miles (370 km). *Endeavour* carried the last permanent US pieces of the station on STS-134, on May 16, 2011.

ZARYA

UNITY

The last ever Shuttle mission, STS-135, was flown by Atlantis on July 8, 2011. It carried a Raffaello module full of supplies. Thirteen days later, the last of the world's heaviest gliders came in hard and fast for the final time at John F. Kennedy Space Center.

RISK FACTORS

R iding hypersonic rockets into space, astronauts must trust in complex, highly engineered machines to transport them safely. On the rare occasions these machines fail, the results can be catastrophic.

Astronaut Vladimir Komarov became the first person killed in spaceflight when the parachute failed on his descending Soyuz 1 capsule, 1967.

STS-51-L, the 25th Shuttle mission, took off with a NASA communications satellite in its payload bay.

BAD PRACTICE

In 1967, *Soyuz 1* was rushed to launch before it was ready. The heat shield had been made heavier and the parachute larger, but the chute holder was left unchanged. The chute was hammered in so tightly it failed to unfurl. Vladimir Komarov was the first space fatality.

STS-51-L crew member Christa McAuliffe waved to onlookers as the crew began their mission.

A similar mix of manufacturing defect and bad practice doomed Space Shuttle *Challenger* on STS-51-L. On January 28, 1986, the subzero temperatures had made an O-ring seal on a joint in the right-hand SRB too brittle. Fifty-eight seconds into launch, burning gas jetted out of the joint, causing a chain reaction that destroyed the Shuttle. The reliability of the O-rings had already been questioned by engineers—but their concerns had not been passed to safety managers.

Flames (circled) burned through the SRB support strut. Seconds later the strut failed, allowing the SRB to strike the external fuel tank and ignite it.

STS-51-L's fuel tank exploded 73 seconds into the flight, causing the orbiter to disintegrate. The crew capsule (circled) was blasted away in one piece but hit the ocean seconds later, killing all on board.

"...reality must take precedence over public relations, for Nature cannot be fooled." Richard Feynman, *Challenger* enquiry

Three astronauts died on reentry in Soyuz 11, 1971, when their capsule depressurized.

FATAL DAMAGE

The investigation into *Challenger* grounded the Shuttle fleet for 32 months. Turnaround time for the fleet was increased. The Shuttle's promise of cheap regular access to orbit was gone.

Commander Rick Husband and pilot William McCool were on Columbia's flight deck just before the accident.

On January 16, 2003, Shuttle *Columbia* rose to begin a mission with the new SpaceHab module. As it lifted, vibration tore a piece of foam loose from the fuel tank that struck the orbiter's left wing. As the mission unfolded in space, flight engineers debated. Was the craft fatally damaged? Probably not. When *Columbia* reentered, hot gases entered a hole in the wing, causing it to fail. *Columbia* tumbled over and broke apart, depressurizing the crew cabin.

Columbia broke up, killing all seven crew. Fragments of the spacecraft were pieced together for the investigation (below)—and the Shuttle's retirement began.

The crew of orbiter Columbia.

HUMAN space **flight** has a **FATALITY RATE** of **roughly 4%**—the **SAME** as **climbing MOUNT EVEREST**.

COMMERCIAL SPACEFLIGHT

SpaceShipOne, the first private spacecraft, used pivoting wings to act like airbrakes, slowing its descent.

Pivoting wings

Rocket

SUB-ORBITAL

O n June 21, 2004, test pilot Mike Melvill flicked the rocket switch on *SpaceShipOne* and screamed to 62 miles (100 km)—the start of space. The era of private spaceflight had arrived.

SpaceShipOne entered space twice more to win the Ansari X-Prize. During each flight, the pilot experienced three and a half minutes of microgravity. The craft was designed by Burt Rutan, an American aeroengineer who also designed the followup, *SpaceShipTwo*.

Rutan's innovations included a hybrid solid/liquid rocket and "piggybacking" the spacecraft to its launch altitude beneath a jet carrier plane "mothership."

SPACESHIPTWO
1. **WHITE KNIGHT TWO**
Twin-fuselage turbofan carrier craft
2. **TURBOFAN ENGINES**
3. **SPACESHIPTWO**
4. **HYBRID ROCKET**

SpaceShipTwo here test fires its rocket engine in 2013.

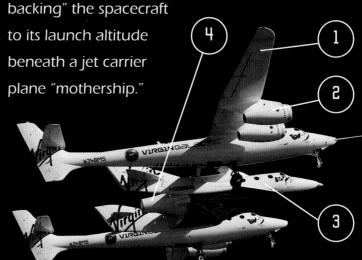

This artist's impression shows the completed Mojave Air & Space Port in California. Virgin Galactic plans to operate a fleet of five SpaceShipTwo craft.

The **COST** of a **PRIVATE SUB-ORBITAL flight** is **EXPECTED** to **be** about $250,000 per **PASSENGER**.

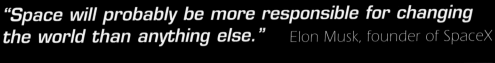

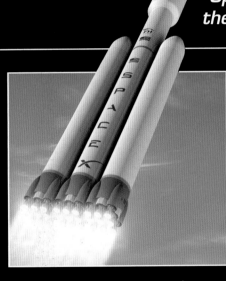

The SpaceX Falcon Heavy is the largest planned commercial heavy-lift rocket. It will raise payloads just under half the size of the retired monster Saturn V, of Apollo fame.

Telecoms mogul Anousheh Ansari was the fourth civilian to pay for a space trip.

SPACE TOURISM

Since 2001, several private individuals have traveled to the ISS aboard Russian Soyuz spacecraft. Space tourism does not come cheap. It involves six months' full astronaut training at Cosmonaut Training Center, Star City, in Russia. The average stay is 10 days, during which the visitor does experiments and takes part in crew activities—perhaps a spacewalk. What is next for the brave pioneers of space travel?

SERVICING THE ISS

Commercial robotic capsules are already being used to resupply the ISS. NASA has awarded funding to three private companies to develop crew vehicles: SpaceX with the *Dragon*, Boeing with its (Apollo-like) CST-100, and Sierra-Nevada Corp's *Dream Chaser* gliding spaceplane.

Dream Chaser is based on the NASA HL-20 spaceplane.

It **COST** Canadian **SPACE TOURIST** Guy Laliberté $40 **MILLION** to **visit** the **ISS** in **2009**.

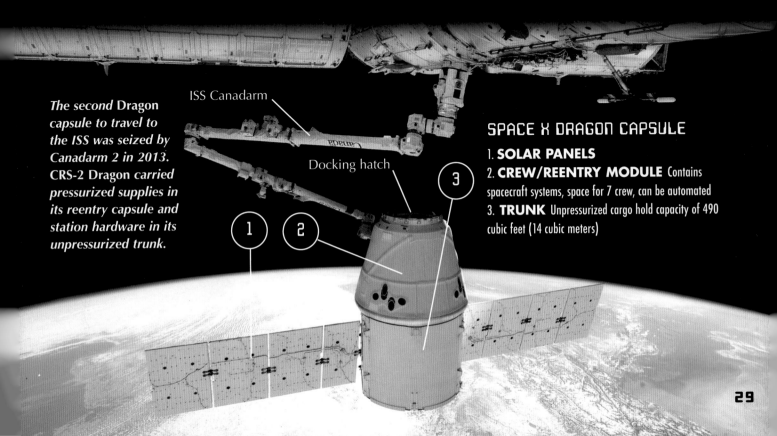

The second Dragon capsule to travel to the ISS was seized by Canadarm 2 in 2013. CRS-2 Dragon carried pressurized supplies in its reentry capsule and station hardware in its unpressurized trunk.

ISS Canadarm

Docking hatch

SPACE X DRAGON CAPSULE

1. **SOLAR PANELS**
2. **CREW/REENTRY MODULE** Contains spacecraft systems, space for 7 crew, can be automated
3. **TRUNK** Unpressurized cargo hold capacity of 490 cubic feet (14 cubic meters)

TECH FILES – SPACE FIRSTS

Excludes Apollo Moon missions

FIRST SUB-ORBITAL VEHICLE
V-2 ROCKET DATE: 1944-45 NATIONALITY: German ALTITUDE: 128 miles (206 km) with maximum long-range trajectory NOTES: Ballistic terror weapon

FIRST ORBITAL VEHICLE
SPUTNIK 1 DATE: October 4, 1957 NATIONALITY: Soviet Union ALTITUDE: 134-583 miles (215-939 km) ORBITS: 1350 NOTES: Experimental satellite

FIRST ANIMAL SPACEFLIGHT
LAIKA DATE: November 3, 1957 NATIONALITY: Soviet Union ALTITUDE: 131-1,031 miles (211-1,659 km) ORBITS: Over 2,000 NOTES: Survived only six orbits

FIRST HUMAN SPACEFLIGHT
YURI GAGARIN DATE: April 12, 1961 NATIONALITY: Soviet Union ALTITUDE: 105-203 miles (169-327 km) ORBITS: One TIME IN SPACE: 1 hour 48 minutes

FIRST SUB-ORBITAL HUMAN SPACEFLIGHT
ALAN SHEPARD DATE: May 5, 1961 NATIONALITY: US ALTITUDE: 101 miles (187.5 km) MISSION DURATION: 15 minutes 22 seconds

FIRST MULTI-CREW SPACEFLIGHT
VOSKHOD 1 DATE: October 12, 1964 NATIONALITY: Soviet Union ALTITUDE: 110-208 miles (178-336 km) ORBITS: 16 CREW: Vladimir Komarov (Commander), Konstantin Feoktistov (Engineer), Boris Yegorov (Doctor) MISSION DURATION: 24 hours 17 minutes

FIRST SPACEWALK
ALEXEY LEONOV DATE: March 18, 1965 NATIONALITY: Soviet Union ALTITUDE: 103-295 miles (167-475 km) EVA DURATION: 12 minutes 9 seconds

FIRST SPACE VEHICLE DOCKING
GEMINI 8 TO AGENA TARGET VEHICLE (ATV) DATE: March 16, 1966 NATIONALITY: US CREW: Neil Armstrong (Commander), David Scott (Pilot) NOTES: Undocked after 31 minutes due to dangerous uncontrolled spinning caused by jammed thrusters on *Gemini 8*

LONGEST HUMAN SPACEFLIGHT
VALERI POLYAKOV DATE BEGUN: January 8, 1994 NATIONALITY: Soviet Union SPACECRAFT: *Mir* TIME IN SPACE: 437 days

FIRST MULTI-PERSON SPACEWALK
YEVGENY KHRUNOV & ALEKSEI YELISEYEV DATE: January 16, 1969 NATIONALITY: Soviet Union MISSIONS: *Soyuz 4 & 5*

LONGEST SPACEWALK
JAMES VOSS & SUSAN HELMS DATE: March 11, 2001 NATIONALITY: US MISSION: STS-102 EVA DURATION: 8 hours 56 minutes NOTES: First of two EVAs to prepare a Pressurized Mating Adapter for relocation onboard the International Space Station

FIRST REUSABLE SPACECRAFT
NASA SPACE SHUTTLE INAUGURAL FLIGHT: STS-1, April 12, 1981, Orbiter *Columbia* FINAL FLIGHT: STS-135, July 21, 2011, Orbiter *Atlantis*

FIRST SPACE TOURIST
DENNIS TITO LAUNCH DATE: April 28, 2001 REENTRY DATE: May 6, 2001 NATIONALITY: US SPACECRAFT: ISS TIME IN SPACE: 7 days 22 hours 4 minutes

GLOSSARY

ATMOSPHERE layer of gases around a space object such as a planet

ATTITUDE position of a spacecraft, for example, its angle in relation to Earth, or pointing at a star

ELLIPTICAL oval-shaped, as for the orbits of many planets and spacecraft

ESCAPE VELOCITY speed needed to get away from an object's gravity, like a moon or planet, and become free in space. For Earth it is 7 miles (11.2 km) per second at the surface

EVA Extra Vehicular Activity, being outside a craft in space, often called a spacewalk

GRAVITY force of attraction between objects, which is especially huge for massive objects like planets and stars

MASS amount of matter in an object, in the form of numbers and kinds of atoms

MICROGRAVITY where the force of gravity from a nearby object, like a planet, is extremely weak or almost zero

MOON space object that orbits a planet. The single moon of Earth is usually known as the Moon (capital letter M)

ORBIT regular path of one object around a larger one, determined by the speed, mass and gravity of the objects

PLANET large space object that has a spherical shape due to its gravity, and has cleared a regular orbital path around a star

REENTRY returning from space to an object such as a planet, when friction with the thickening atmosphere slows the spacecraft but also causes immense heat

RETROROCKETS rockets facing the direction of motion of a craft, fired to slow it down

SATELLITE space object that goes around or orbits another, including natural satellites like the Moon orbiting Earth or Earth orbiting the Sun, and man-made satellites

STAR space object that at some stage is large and dense enough, with enough gravity, to undergo fusion and give out light, heat, and similar energy

SUB-ORBITAL a mission that leaves the surface of a planet, flies into space, then comes down again, instead of going into orbit

INDEX